senior moments

*Prayer-talks with God
about aging grace-fully*

Bernadette McCarver Snyder

**TWENTY-THIRD
PUBLICATIONS**
twentythirdpublications.com

Fifth Printing 2018

TWENTY-THIRD PUBLICATIONS
One Montauk Avenue, Suite 200, New London, CT 06320
(860) 437-3012 » (800) 321-0411 » www.twentythirdpublications.com

Cover photo: ©iStockphoto.com/ChrisBaynham

ISBN: 978-1-62785-033-9
Library of Congress Catalog Card Number: 2014940877
Printed in the U.S.A.

 A division of Bayard, Inc.

DEDICATION

Hope is the thing with feathers
that perches in the soul
and sings the tune
without the words
and never stops at all.
EMILY DICKINSON

If you keep a green tree
within your heart
I have heard,
One day, there will come to stay
A singing bird.
ANON

With these two favorite quotations,
I dedicate this book to all ninrn who have
"moments," and the brave way they keep
hope and music in their hearts.

Where are you?

Time is precious, possibly even more so when you
have enough years to have accumulated a lot of
happy "remember whens" and maybe a few "I can't
remember whats." Everyone alive is aging, no matter what age they are. So join the club. Appreciate
the perks of seniority. Be grateful for the gift of
each day. And whenever you are having a "senior
moment," do a bit of praying!

There's a saying: "pray always"; and you *can* do
that if you just pray wherever you go, whatever
you are doing, whether it's a great day or a sad day.
You can make the most of whatever is happening
in your life by turning it *all* into prayer time.

This little book will give you ideas of the way
you might pray *wherever you are*.

Get a life?

Dear Lord, here I am in my cozy kitchen, brewing up a cup of tea to warm the cockles of my aging heart. Yes, I said aging, not fully aged yet. I could have mellowed like a fine wine or aged cheese— but I didn't. I still sometimes make decisions as silly as I did as a teenager or act as moody as a middle-aged "mad housewife," but today I am just a bit crotchety because I started remembering a time when my aging was attacked.

I had pulled into a parking spot a bit crookedly, so I needed to back out a bit and then go back in to get parked perfectly. It only took a few seconds, but it obviously irritated the sweet young person who was waiting to pull around me, so she stuck her head out of her car window and yelled, "Get a life!"

Lord, I have had a life—and what a wonderful one it has been. A lot of years have come and gone, full of fun and folly, glad, sad, and glorious. And I thank you for each and every day. I still have a life, but one that is a bit different, a bit "challenged" at times. I can still do most of my favorite things, maybe not quite as fast and probably not quite as well, but so what? I've been there, done that, in the old days. Now it's time to keep from getting discouraged by looking for new ways to do old routines—take shortcuts, simplify expectations, pay someone to do the big lifting and big chores, etc.

By downsizing the work load and clearing out some of the gotta-dos, I thought I might find time to do things I never had time to do before. I searched and found my old "wish list," but it's a bit dated. I don't think it's time now for me to go sky-diving or find a cure for speed-sneezing.

Lord, I think maybe you might be telling me to use my "found" time to learn to be less anxious about the inconvenience of aging, less hesitant to try new ways to adapt, and then learn to be more grateful for each new day. Recently I heard that the trick to staying alive and lively is "to find something you really love to work on or be a part of," so I think that will be #2 on my NEW wish list. Of course, #1 will be to spend more time in prayer-visits, happy remembrances, laughing at my own foolishness, and seeing problems as an opportunity to learn. Then all my senior moments can be filled with more peace and less angst.

Thanks, Lord, for my crazy life, both past and present, but I gotta go now—my tea is getting cold.

When in a fog

Dear Lord, I'm feeling a bit foggy today. I have things to do, but I don't want to do them. I have places to go, but I want to just sit here with my cup of coffee and wait for the fog to clear.

But I began thinking of that time I was driving home from Tennessee and hit a patch of fog on the highway. It felt like somebody had thrown a blanket over my windshield. I was so scared. I wanted to pull over and stop, but I couldn't even tell where the side of the road was. And then, just before I panicked, I saw a red light, a taillight, in front of me. I knew I was not alone. I hoped the driver in front was better at fogginess than I was, and I kept following that taillight until I could see a big exit sign. Then I carefully exited and came upon a cluster of stores where there was a fast-food place. I sheltered there with a cup of coffee, just like today, waiting for the fog to clear. Then I got back on the highway and hit blue skies on the way home.

You know, Lord, when one gets a bit older, people start looking at you suspiciously, wondering if you are getting foggy with your thinking. It is not a happy feeling when younger and "wiser" heads question your invaluable, extremely intelligent, and positively correct advice. They totally ignore the fact that they too are sometimes a bit foggy, especially in early mornings. So help me, Lord, to make peace with their impatience and with mine.

Remind me I am not alone. In the past, you have always been that light that led me out of a fog, and I am so grateful for that. Be my light today. Help me clear out my foggy head and help me get the things to do, done, and the places to go, gone. And if I get tired and need to rest, show me an exit sign so I can rest and refuel. Then, Lord, get me back on the road—with blue skies on my way home.

On a stormy day

Dear Lord, did you recently choose someone new to be in charge of the weather? Things have gotten out of control all over the place. I can't remember a time when the news was so full of storms, tornadoes, hurricanes, floods, and snow in unexpected parts of the planet. I'm grateful that my hometown weather has been pleasant, even if totally unpredictable. I look out in the morning and all is stormy, so I layer myself to be rainproof and warm. But by the time I am ready to leave, the sun has come out shining on me and probably laughing at my outfit.

I know this is a trivial thing to be bothering you about, but I am, because this strange unpredictable weather seems to be a symptom of today's world—all mixed up. We used to have some standards in our world, not all good or all bad, but we knew what to expect and what to count on. Now, as we slowly age into uncertainty, we need something stable, something we can count on and depend on. And yes, I know we already have what we need and that is *you*. Sorry, Lord, if I bothered you by mentioning this, but you know well that I too am sometimes unpredictable. And it gets worse when everything around me is changing, "improving," confusing, and downright scary.

Well, I've had my say, and I feel better now. But I do hope you will check on your weather guru. All the weather professionals here on earth seem to spend lots of time telling me to expect rain when I can look out the window and see that it *is* raining. Now, of course, I have to remember they are just human, so they are bound to get it wrong sometimes, just like I do in everyday life.

Thank you, Lord, for weather predictors who probably do the best they can. And thank you for the excitement of thunderstorms and the soothing peace of gentle rains and the awesome beauty of a first snowfall and the greening miracle of spring. But thank you most for being my umbrella through all kinds of weather, both fair and foul.

Puzzling

Dear Lord, some people like bingo or maybe hang gliding; some like the seashore or possibly mountain climbing; some like opera music; and others like soap operas. Some like same old, same old, and others are always ready to try something new. So I am puzzled why some younger people forget that seniors are people! They think all seniors are pretty much alike. They think that once you become a certain age, you should "act your age." Well, OK, some elders enjoy doing just that. But others have different plans—as different as the clues in a crossword puzzle.

I mention that, because crossword puzzles are one of *my* likes and one of my time-user-uppers. I love finding strange new words and their meanings in the crossword clues. For example, I learned that the word *gephyrophobia* is the fear of crossing bridges. I may never be able to use that word in a conversation, but I'm glad to know I don't have the phobia, since, as I age, I keep having new bridges to cross.

Lord, I don't know why, but when I am stressed or worried or come to a new bridge, I can shut off the world and sit down to puzzle out all the answers. And when I get all the words in their proper places, I feel I have accomplished something.

Another reason I love crosswords is because they have been around since who-knows-when. I always look forward to solving the daily puzzle in the newspaper, and I think I heard that it was around 1913 when a crossword puzzle first appeared in a newspaper—the *New York Sunday World*. As today's world is so changing and often puzzling (to many but especially to seniors), it soothes me to know that something in my world is older than I am.

Because so many things that I enjoyed and treasured have been discontinued, I am aware that newspapers are an endangered species and I may lose my daily dose of crossed words, but this time I have a backup. A good friend gave me a book full of *New York Times* Sunday puzzles. The book is so big it may outlast me *and* the newspapers.

So, Lord, thanks for friends bearing gifts, and thanks for seniors and all their differences. Thank you for the fun of my puzzle "pass-time," and thank you that I will never have to puzzle whether you will be there when I call. I know you will.

When using the dreaded four-letter words

Dear Lord, there are some four-letter words I really hate. I want to wipe them from my vocabulary, but I can't. They keep showing up, disrupting my days and even my nights. They intrude on my fun times and my quiet times. Those four-letter words—dust, cook, tidy, iron—cannot be ignored, no matter how hard I try.

Actually, I have managed to ignore that last one, because my iron has been sitting unused on a shelf ever since I discovered those beautiful, wonderful, four-letter words—wash and wear.

And I guess "tidy" may not be a proper four-letter word, but it comes to my mind because I have so much practice "tidying" the house when it's time for someone to drop by. Frantically I gather up the coupons I've been clipping and throw them into a drawer, possibly not to be seen again until they have expired. Then I gather up the stack of newspapers and magazines that I meant to read last night and I stash them in the garage. And I throw anything left in the kitchen into the dishwasher and close the door. Some people keep house by having a place for everything and everything in its place. But the things in my house don't seem to know their "place."

You may have noticed, Lord, that today I came in the house, dropped my coat on a chair, left my keys on the table, unloaded the groceries onto the kitchen counter, brought in the mail and the newspaper and dropped them by my easy chair, and got a cup of tea. But then I sat it down when the phone rang, telling me that a friend was on the way over. Then I looked at my house and saw that I needed to tidy up—immediately.

Well, Lord, we had a nice visit, compared our current aches and pains, criticized the government, made plans to go somewhere nice for lunch next week, and shared the latest news from the grandchildren. So now all I have to do is wipe up the cookie crumbs and throw away the tea bags and get something out of the freezer for dinner. But I'll get back to you, Lord, hopefully with a better, less frazzled "tidied up" prayer.

At church

Dear Lord, I always felt comfortable in my parish church. It wasn't historic or fantastically beautiful or designed dramatically, but I felt at home there. Then, as you know, a parishioner decided to donate money to be used for putting in stained-glass windows. I had seen such windows in many churches when I traveled, and they were very inspiring, so I thought that it would be wonderful to see them every time I went to my church. The artisans worked a long time installing them, but when the windows were finished, I cannot say that I was happy.

They were not beautiful. Jesus and the apostles and everybody in the design of the windows were—excuse me for saying this—ugly.

They had long faces and really big, naked, ugly feet. Shouldn't they at least have sandals, since they were always walking somewhere? And all the straggly hair and beards did not help. But the colors WERE bright and beautiful, and on a sunny morning they sparkled and cast brilliant shadows across the church.

I kept trying to look at the windows and find inspiration, and finally I realized that each depicted a special spiritual event. I began to see the lessons that they had been trying to tell me. There was one window that I actually began to like. Of all the hundreds of pieces of stained glass there was *one* piece in this window that was round and white and solid—not see-through. The sun did not shine through it, so you couldn't miss it. My eye was drawn to it. It was a host that Jesus was holding up, saying, "This is my body." The host was solid, real, there to feed us. And Jesus was the light.

Well, Lord, as usual it took me a while to get the message. And it wasn't because I am getting old. It was because I was stupid at first, just like when I was young. So thank you, Lord, for continuing to send me messages even when it takes me a while to see them. Help me to welcome them and cherish them so that maybe I won't be like the old German expression, "too soon old, too late smart."

New warning labels

Lord, I'm in danger today. I've put it off as long as I can, but today I *have* to clean out my cluttered kitchen pantry. Every time I open the door, I am in danger of being clobbered by an enraged can of beans or an indignant package of pasta falling off the shelf. It's all because of the new warning labels that now appear on all foodstuffs. In the past, I could ignore my pantry, but now I know everything in there has a "best by" or "use by" date that may soon expire. If I wait until I find labels that have expired, I will have to throw them out and feel guilty because I let them go unused and unappreciated too long.

Lord, in the past I always stocked up when there was a sale, so I was never sure how long which can had been sitting there waiting to be used. Every time I chose an item, I had to make a decision—whether to throw it out or endanger my life by eating it. Now I know. Cooking isn't as exciting as it used to be, but I should be grateful that someone is watching out for me.

I've been thinking about whether I and other elders may have a "use by" date too. If we do, we should do something about that. While we are sitting around eating chocolates and watching TV, maybe we have already gone past the "best by" label, but we could still be aware of the "use by" and get out and do some volunteer work or write a letter to an old friend or cook lunch or dinner for someone (using perfectly labeled ingredients only).

Yes, Lord, it's not good to have a cluttered pantry or life. We should get organized and be aware that we should use whatever ability we still have left. We could try to help someone or cheer someone or even pray for someone before our "use by" label expires. There are so many more opportunities today for seniors to get out and get into activities that help others and ourselves. And they are a lot more fun than just sitting on the shelf waiting for someone to come check our labels.

Only say the word

Dear Lord, when I said that part of the Communion prayer today—"only say the word and my soul shall be healed"—I began to think how "only a word" can change a life.

It only takes a word to answer questions like, "Will you marry me?" or "Could you start the new job on Monday?" or "Could you invite an exchange student to live in your home for a school year?" or even "Can we get a dog?"

Looking back through the years, there were quite a few questions that made a big life change for me—and probably for many others—depending on the answers.

Lord, I seldom can think of a clever reply when someone asks a clever question—until the next day when the proper answer dawns on me—but I certainly recall times when my answer to a question truly changed my life. I am so grateful I said yes to marriage and to the new job that brought me to a new city where I met the guy who proposed the marriage. I never had the opportunity to host an exchange student, and I'm sorry I missed that. But I did get a dog and later a cat, and they each changed my life in a good way.

There have been times when I said yes and should have said no, or no when I should have said yes. And there have been lots of times when that happened at a garage sale and I came home with you-wouldn't-believe-what. But there were also important questions that I wish I had answered with a different word, and I guess we all have those times to remember and regret.

And, Lord, I know there is one word, the Bible, that I should have spent more time studying. I still have time to do that, so I will start on it right away, just as soon as I get finished with all the things I promised to take care of right away and all the chores on my to-do list. OK, Lord, forgive my procrastination. I really will do better and take time to learn all those good words in your word. I promise. Soon. Maybe.

Memories...

Dear Lord, for anyone of a certain age (and we know who we are), visiting our memories can be a lovely respite or a sad discovery. Experts tell us that anyone who qualifies for a senior discount (and that's anyone over 50!) may have a memory that is already slipping in speed and accuracy. If they are right, then just when you have conquered a lot of life's problems and are "living in the moment," you might find that it is a "senior moment"!

But wait! Some scientists have not bought into the idea of "age-related cognitive decline." Some linguistic researchers realized that most educated older people generally know more words than younger people just because they've lived more years. So using different kinds of memory "tests" and facing the fact that some people remain amazingly sharp-witted into their 90s, they are considering a different idea about memories. They say that when it takes an older person longer to come up with a word or a memory, it's because they have a "larger library" in their head; so naturally it takes a bit longer to search through it!

Lord, I like the way these younger scientists

think. Unless they are just making up excuses *now* that they can use *later* when they too are getting senior discounts as well as "moments."

Well, Lord, whoever and whatever is correct in this "diagnosis," taking time out for happy memories is still a pleasant pastime for seniors. So we can give thanks for that. And when we have a "lapse" while looking for the right word, now we can think of our big "in-head, in-house" library and say, "It's not because seniors are slow. It's just because we know so much!"

Do you think we can get away with that, Lord?

If the shoe fits

Dear Lord, you might be shocked to hear that I am wearing a ninety-dollar pair of shoes. Don't worry. You know I didn't pay ninety dollars. I had heard of a store where they sell the "reject" clothes from a very fancy, expensive store, so I decided to check it out yesterday. That was a mistake, because they were having a big shoe sale, and I actually found a ninety-dollar pair of shoes that fit just right and had been reduced to a low-enough price that I wouldn't have to feel guilty about buying them! So here I am, dancing about, pretending I am the Queen of Sheba, or at least someone who normally wears ninety-dollar shoes.

Of course, Lord, I know I should not be taking your time to talk about something so trivial. But I tell you all my bad news every day, so it just seemed right that I should tell you some good news today.

It's not really big news like winning a trip to Hawaii or losing five pounds or making a really good pie crust, but it is good enough to jingle my bell and remind me I should be pulling out weeds in the garden instead of checking out new stores.

Also, I should be taking time to think about and pray for the seniors I know who used to jog and dance and run hither and there, but are now limping around with painful knees that make it hard to walk. I should pray today for those who are in rehab doing exercises to get their stride back or those who now travel by wheelchair.

So many of them never let anything get them down. They keep on keeping on, never complaining and being an inspiration to us all. Bless them, Lord.

When I have lost control

Dear Lord, I was so comfortable in my cozy little house with the antique décor and potted plants and doodads here and there. But then I lost control—not because I got old, but because my son decided to drag me into the uncomfortable world of technology.

I had a perfectly nice TV that was friendly. Now I have a new one, a bigger one, one that I don't really know how to operate. I also have a new DVD player that keeps spitting out discs because I pushed the wrong button. I even have a new refrigerator that has a helpful ice-maker, but every time it starts popping out cubes late at night it sounds like someone trying to break into the house. But that's OK, because I know no robber is near, because I have a new security system that shrieks to high heaven if anyone touches a door or window. Oh, and my new telephone has a menu/ select, a talk/flash, a redial/pause, a message/mute, an intercom/clear— and a strange looking "Icon" to identify each one. I have lost control.

Some days I feel like I am back in kindergarten, just learning the ABCs of a language I thought I already knew. I am told it is good for an old brain to learn new things. I am told you just need to pay attention. But how can I pay attention to so many new things so fast? Oh Lord, I admit that I am learning, but what I am learning is how to complain, complain, instead of how to adapt, adapt.

Lord, I do want to be "with it" and up to date, and I know I should try harder. I should remember that my foremothers went from big, black, iron skillets and wood stoves to microwave ovens, from handmade brooms to motorized vacuum cleaners, from sputtering candlelight to lasers, from horse and buggies to space flights. Why am I complaining?

So help me, Lord, to be willing to try to learn about this new world. It can be embarrassing to feel so stupid about things even children take for granted. It can be depressing to even take notes about what to do and then still do it wrong. But, Lord, it has taken me a lifetime trying to learn about *your* world of mysteries and miracles, and I'm still taking notes and studying and paying attention and rejoicing at every new little bit you reveal to me. So thank you, Lord, for being patient with me and for being such a good teacher.

When I am lonely

Well, here I am, Lord, all sad and lonely, blue and boredly. I have friends, but this week no one calls, no one visits. I have good neighbors, but they have recently been listed as missing and out of action. What happened? I used to be popular, with people always inviting me places, asking for my advice, telling me funny stories. But today, they are too busy to worry about me and my miseries.

Yes, Lord, I know this is one of those days when I sink into my own pit of pity and am too lazy to start digging my way out. Of course, I also know I should do *something* to change things. I could write a letter to someone who is probably lonelier than I am. I could call a chatty friend just to hear another voice. Even better, Lord, maybe I should look in the mirror and say, "Who *are* you?"

Then I should ask, "Why are you sitting there feeling all poor and sorely and mad at the world, thinking someone else, anyone else, is responsible for your boredom? You know that no matter how old or how prickly you get, *you* are the one responsible for your own loneliness." But wait a minute, Lord, I don't want to do that. I *want* to blame someone else. In fact, Lord, you'd better watch out! Today, I am so down and out, I am even thinking of blaming *you* for my loneliness.

Well, enough of that. I know my friends and neighbors are just busy today—and I should be too! I still have a bit of grit left to want to get up and *do* some digging so I can appreciate the precious gift of today. Actually, I'm feeling better now, Lord, since you have listened again and whispered into my ear to tell me to look around and see that I have more things to be thankful for and less things to worry about than a lot of my friends do. I have a bed to sleep in, a cup of tea when I want one, and even this bit of quiet time when I don't have to be busy and can spend it with you.

How can I be so stupid as to be lonely, when here I am with you, the best consoler, the best gift-giver, the best listener in the world?

In a doctor's office

Dear Lord, here I am in another doctor's office.
They are all so different and still the same. Some
are too small and the patients are all seated too
close together, so when someone starts sharing
their medical history, others chime in—and some
wish they wouldn't. Or the office is very comfortable and luxurious—and you start wondering
if you will be able to afford this doctor if he has
splurged so much money on his office.

I have spent a lot of time in these places through
the years, either waiting with my husband for his
appointments or waiting for my own. I should be
accustomed to it by now, but I still get the pitty-
pats wondering what the outcome will be.

Thank you, Lord; I didn't have to wait long
today, and then I heard what I had hoped to hear.
First, the physician's assistant told me I looked
younger than my age. That was probably his way
of cheering me up. But then we got down to the
"answer." I did not hear that all is well. The X-ray
was not a pretty picture. But then I was told that if
I follow a simple therapy regimen, it will at least
not get worse and I can continue doing all the

crazy things I like to do. At my age, that was music to my ears—just what I wanted to hear.

Now as I am waiting to get the printout of my report, I am looking around at the others in the office. Some look sad or mad, probably wondering why this illness or accident happened to them. Some are laughing with the nurse, leaving with a good report, as I will. So I pray, Lord, that you will reach out to them all, comforting those who need it today, staying close to those who are facing a long recuperation, and calming the pitty-pats of others. And I especially thank you, Lord, that I have found a doctor I trust. I ask you to help me be a worthy patient.

Now I'm outa here, Lord, on my way to step back into my world, rejoicing in the sunny day and my old car that is waiting to whisk me away with the prospect of happy surprises around the next corner.

When I need a smile

Dear Lord, today I needed a smile—and I found one. I was looking through a book of poems, and I found one that just fit my mood. The poet who wrote it was the famous "Anon," and here it is:

May the light always find you on a dreary day,
When you need to be home, may you find a way.
May you always have courage to take a chance
And never find frogs in your underpants.

Yep, that's just what I needed to hear today. It was the light I needed on a dreary day. And I was already at home, so I didn't have to find a way. And so far, I really never have found frogs in my underpants, so that only leaves finding courage to take a chance.

And as I age, Lord, that is not as easy as it once was.

When I was a fair, young thing, Lord, you know I was offered a job in a new city, a place where I knew no one except the people at the company that offered me the job. I jumped at the chance, packed my little, old, blue Dodge with some clothes and an old typewriter, and took off. And it changed my life happily ever after.

It was a fun job in advertising, writing radio and TV commercials. And I made new friends and found a new best friend in the office next to mine, and she talked me into going with her to tour Europe for three weeks, the dream trip of a lifetime for me. Then, a few years later, on a snowy morning, I met a handsome young man while waiting for a streetcar. And we got married and went clang, clang, clang together ever after. But of course, you know all this, Lord. I am just wandering as usual. But having had such good luck when I had the courage to take a chance, I know I should never hesitate. But I do. Old age has different meanings about taking chances.

Now I have to be prudent and not wear the spike-heel shoes that made me taller and took me all over Europe. I can't just grab my computer and dash off to a new city or even dash outside on snowy mornings. But I still have the courage to keep writing books and taking a chance that someone will enjoy reading them.

And at this age, I guess I'm still waiting for The Streetcar named Retire.

When in danger

Dear Lord, my neighborhood is in danger. A masked bandit has invaded our territory. He strikes at night, stealing everything he can reach. The neighbors have set traps and alarms, but the bandit outsmarts them all. The worst part is that the bandit is so cute, staring at you through his little mask while he uses his little hands to tear into your garbage bags and throw the contents all over your yard. Yes, Lord, the bandit is a raccoon.

Of course, you know, Lord, it's all your fault. You made this critter look cute (and humans do like cute) by adding that face mask, but he wasn't made to live in a subdivision. And it's not his fault he ended up here, so one of the guys finally got a cage to trap the bandit and drove him out by a river and let him out to roam so he can find food without looking for it in a black plastic garbage bag.

While the neighbors were all wringing their hands and cleaning their yards, I looked up a bit about the raccoon. It seems that if a raccoon lives near a stream or any kind of water, he likes to dip his food in the water—like washing his food before he eats. Again, so cute! But scientists think he just does that because he likes wet food better than dry.

I can identify with that. Sometimes I like to dip a donut in my coffee, or a strawberry in melted chocolate, or a healthy celery stick into a calorie-laden cheesy, yummy, handmade dip. But I'm not very cute at it, so again I am in danger, because the coffee drips down my chin, or the chocolate drips down to stain my sweater, or the dip gets all over my fingers. Unlike the raccoon, I am not a pretty sight.

Well, Lord, thank you for today, when the danger of the rascally raccoon tearing up the neighborhood has passed us by and we will have to find some other topic to talk about over the fence or the phone. And thank you, Lord, that we are blessed to live in a safe, friendly neighborhood. Watch over all those who truly are in danger in war-torn countries or war-torn neighborhoods or even war-torn families. Remind us all to be truly grateful and to always pray for those less blessed than we are.

When it's cookbook time

Dear Lord, here I am in the kitchen again. But this time I am seeking guidance at my kitchen bookshelf. It is stuffed with all kinds of cookbooks, some bought at church suppers, some from cute little bookstores or at restaurants offering their own special recipes. Sometimes I just thumb through the pages, trying to remember where I was or whom I was with when I got one book or another. Sometimes I like to read elegant recipes that promise to help me turn out gourmet meals at a moment's notice.

For example, today I found a great recipe I could cook for dinner tonight—if I had a large rib roast, a pound of asparagus, some fresh mushrooms, a bunch of herbs, and a bottle of brandy. But I don't, and I won't anytime soon, so I kept looking. What I really need is just to find a new way to cook whatever I can dig up in the fridge or freezer.

Then, while thumbing, I came across some food trivia. I learned that the word *wonton* is Chinese for "swallowing a cloud" and *nacho* is Spanish for "flat-nosed." See how it is with my life,

Lord? I start out looking for a simple recipe and instead find how to swallow a cloud!

I would like to know how it feels to swallow a cloud, but, as usual, I don't have the right ingredients on hand for making wontons. I think I can manage nachos, so I guess I'll have to settle for a flat-nosed dinner tonight.

Sorry, Lord, I got carried away and took a detour to ponder, as I usually do when I start thumbing through any book, even a cookbook. But I thank you, Lord, for my cozy kitchen, for books to read and dinners to cook and the fun of trivia. Now again, Lord, help me find a good recipe for my days, with just the right amount of searching and learning and appreciating, with a cupful of laughter stirred lovingly in.

Making an impression

Dear Lord, I probably should be seeking and welcoming change, but some days the "same old, same old" seems so comfortable that I don't even want to talk about change—until something appears to challenge me.

I like to go to the same old grocery where I know how to find the meat and potatoes and bread and milk, but they keep adding things. These days, most groceries also have a pharmacy, a deli, flu shots, a flower shop, an aisle filled with greeting cards, etc., etc. I have adjusted to this, but today I heard that some groceries now have fingerprint-imaging machines. You can "register" by placing one of your fingers on an electronic screen. The machine registers a digital imprint of your fingerprint and then, whenever you buy groceries, you can pay for them with check, cash, credit card—or fingerprint!

I've often said the FBI would love my house because it's full of fingerprints. Now my grocery may soon be full of fingerprints too!

Lord, when you gave each of us our very own, very personal fingerprints, did you expect us to use them to buy groceries? I think maybe you might have expected us to use them to make an impression on the world around us, to set an example for others by following your commandments, to change somebody's life by giving them a chuckle or a hug or a hand up when they most need one.

Well, I guess those are "same old, same olds" that we should continue to do anyway. And the grocery store change is totally trivial compared to all the changes that sneak up on seniors. So forgive me, Lord, for making a big thing out of a small change, for wasting a dollar's worth of time on a change that's only a nickle's worth. Show me how to adjust, accept, and get over it when an important or necessary change comes along. And help me, Lord, to leave *your* fingerprints wherever I go today—and all the days to come.

When negotiating

Dear Lord, when I was younger, I was always negotiating with you. I'd pray, and then I'd begin to
bargain. If you would send someone to invite me
to the prom, I would give up candy and sweets for
a month. If you would help me get the job I was
applying for, I would promise to set the alarm and
always be on time for work. If you would help
me find the right husband, an affordable house, a
new doctor, an old friend, or a solution for whatever was "happening" in my life, I would think
of something to offer in return. You must have
thought I was crazy, but you forgave me because I
was young and didn't understand the proper way
to pray.

Now, Lord, I am old and you still forgive me
for being stupid.

I know now that "negotiating" is not listed in
the "proper" ways to pray—humbly asking for
help when I need it, saying sorry for something I
did and shouldn't have, thanking you for so many
blessings, and praising you always for the beauty
and miracles I see everywhere in the world you
made for me to discover and appreciate.

But, Lord, even after all the years of trying to pray like an adult should, I am still tempted to bargain. I still want to say: if you give me this, I'll do that; if you overlook my latest mistake, I'll never ever do it again. Yes, Lord, I am in my third childhood, still wanting you to kiss it and make it well.

I know Noah didn't negotiate. He just went to work and built the ark, even though it didn't seem like a good idea at the time. Mary didn't negotiate like mothers often do with children. Without offering a payback, she simply asked for the miracle of water turning into wine.

So, Lord, I guess the one thing I can offer in return for your friendship is to promise to give up negotiating!

When feeling unhappy

Dear Lord, today I was looking through a book
that had lots of wise sayings in it. One of them advised, "Happiness is an inside job." Oh, how well I
know that. Another reminded, "The only way out
is through."

Well, Lord, there are wise sayings everywhere.
You can find wise sayings in the Bible and in
books written by people who have "been there."
Even one's family and friends sometimes come
up with wise advice about unhappiness. But that
doesn't mean one can immediately be cured by
just hearing wise words. In my many years, I have
learned that you have to let yourself really be
open to thinking about how those words apply to
you and how you can act on them.

Lord, whenever I had an unhappy time in the
past, I was absolutely sure that it would never get
better. I was sadder than any of my friends ever
had been, so how could I expect them to understand? I was a victim. I didn't deserve such bad
luck. I was hopeless and helpless.

But you helped me, Lord, to give up the poor-
little-me act and work to get the happiness back

inside. It wasn't always easy or pleasant but you kept reminding me that the only way out is through.

I know now that life happens. And every story does not have a happy ending. But I have learned to look for the humor and find something to laugh about in the midst of any misery. Of course, as you know, Lord, I am still not always Little Miss Sunshine. But you and I keep working on it.

When I look in the mirror

Dear Lord, mornings can be disastrous. One has
to be careful. It's not good for your health to look
too carefully too early in the mirror. Unless, of
course, you need that shock to get your clock ticking enough to face the day. Of course, my clock is
not the digital type. It is the old wind-up model,
and sometimes in the morning I really need to get
rewound or even reset.

The old face and body should be reason for
rejoicing—just because they have lasted so long.
Instead, some of us keep blaming them for not
looking as perfect as the senior models we see on
TV. Instead of making fun of what we've got left,
we might need to give it a rest—let the poor old
things relax and heal from the constant stress of
being criticized.

And, of course, Lord, the mind is the important part of the problem. I guess I'm luckier than
many. My life's purpose was never to be Miss
America or Mrs. Hardware Store. I knew I was
out of the running before the running started. I
just hoped to look presentable, and even that was
not always easy. I never knew if I was wearing the

right thing or saying the right thing at the right time. But that still hasn't stopped me from "seeking enlightenment," signing up for classes to learn whatever somebody was teaching, and stopping to take big gulps of each day, even though it might be impolite.

So thank you, Lord, for the kind of mirrors I needed and found—the role models who have fought the fight and won the race and shown me how to make the most out of whatever comes along. I know, Lord, that you are the best role model, and I'll never stop asking your advice and talking to you about my problems and possibilities—but sometimes, Lord, I also need to seek advice from somebody who talks back.

Dear Lord, as old as I am, you would think that I had already learned enough to get by. But, surprisingly, I keep learning things I never thought about before. Just this morning, I learned that you have to work fast to enjoy breakfast cereal!

When I was growing up, we never had boxed cereal. We had hot oatmeal or hot biscuits with butter and jelly or cinnamon toast or maybe bacon and eggs to go with it. Yes, my mom did know how to start the day off right.

When I went away to find a new job in a new city and live in a new apartment, Lord, you know I almost never had my mother's idea of breakfast. I was lucky to grab a cup of coffee and maybe a quick boiled egg or a rare donut treat, but still no cold cereal. After I got married, my husband sometimes had a bowl of cereal, but I was never interested.

Now that I live alone, I am trying new things (alert the media!). The grocery had a special on this cereal that is supposed to be good for cholesterol, and it tastes like honey and looks like teeny-tiny donuts. Maybe I was lured by the thought of any kind of donuts, so I decided to try some.

Since I no longer have to rush off to an office, I can have a lazy breakfast, so I often get settled in my easy chair and turn on the morning TV news before I take a bite. I had tasted the cereal after I poured on the milk and it was crunchy and delicious. But I did not know there was a time limit before it would turn into a soggy mush. Now I know you have to munch fast if you want crunch.

See, Lord: among my many senior discoveries, I have now learned a new way to eat breakfast— fast! I know there are so many new things being discovered today, marvels of the universe and the mysterious world of computers, but who knew I could speed up my life with a bowl of cereal! Thanks, Lord. How sweet it is!

When feeling low

Dear Lord, you could say I am always feeling low these days. That's because in my former life I was taller! I was actually only five feet three inches tall, but I always wore those spiky high-heeled shoes that gave me another couple of inches. In the last few years, Lord, you may have noticed that I have become the suprisingly shrinking woman. Not only did I lose at least three bodily inches, but for once I decided to be practical and finally gave up the spikes. Now I wear shoes that are as low to the ground as possible so that I won't fall and break the old bones. Before I always felt I was standing tall. Now my stature is ruining my status.

How can people look up to me when I am short enough to have to look up to some first-graders? I take along a pillow so that I won't have to ask for a booster seat in restaurants (but they still won't let me order from the kids menu).

Well, Lord, that's enough venting. I never expected anybody to look up to me anyway, but I never felt low either. I have felt old, but not low, or at least not very low.

I found out a long time ago that you can stop

feeling low by doing something to "change the world." You can make brownies for a lonely neighbor, offer to take a shut-in for a ride to a mall or a movie, get a take-out meal and take it to a widow or widower, help out at a soup kitchen, or do whatever you can find to do to change your world, at least for a while.

Lord, I know this sounds easier than it is, but I've tried these little things, and they changed me—and hopefully those I surprised—if not the world at large. I am still low down in height, but whenever I feel a low feeling coming on, I get out and do something; and then I look up to you and change that low to hello!

When autumn leaves...

Dear Lord, gathering up the autumn leaves is really a big chore (which I now pay someone else to do), but I hate to see the leaves leave because then winter is just waiting to send snow to take their place. And snow is not usually a senior's friend. But this morning I went out to put a letter in the box, and when I lifted the little red flag to remind the post person to stop, I saw a lovely golden leaf had wedged itself behind the flag. It looked like a flower tucked in a man's lapel. And that made me think of my grandfather.

In an honored place in my family room, there is a photo of him when he must have been a senior citizen too. He is sitting ramrod straight, wearing his best suit and tie, looking sternly but with a twinkle in his eye; and there is a little flower in his lapel. He was gone before I was born, so I never knew him, but when I see that flower, I think he had a bit of fun in him like I do. I have heard feisty stories of my grandpa, and he even made a grand exit.

When Grandpa's obit appeared in the Nashville, Tennessee, newspaper, it explained that Squire McCarver had been visiting his daughter in

Jackson, Tennessee, when he died of a heart attack, but he would be buried in Bell Buckle, Tennessee. On the way there, his casket would arrive in Nashville by train at 10 AM Saturday morning— and friends should pay their respects to the family at the Union Station! I'm pretty sure none of my friends had a grandpa whose wake was at a railroad station!

Well, Lord, family stories often bring strange memories, and happy ones too, to remind us of our interesting roots. So today, Lord, I'm thinking of my colorful family and also enjoying the beautiful colors you have used to paint the autumn leaves. I remember a line from Albert Camus: "Autumn is a second spring where every leaf is a flower." So thank you, Lord, for today's beautiful leaf-flowers and especially for the one on the mailbox that triggered memories of my Southern grandpa, Squire McCarver.

Watching the weather

Dear Lord, I always heard that lightning never strikes the same place twice. Today I came across a little book that indicated that this is not true. It reported that there is a church in England that has been struck by lightning 152 times! And then there's the Empire State Building in New York City, where lightning hits on an average of twenty-three times a year. Well, I've been on the top of that New York wonder, and it is so high up in the sky that lightning wouldn't have to travel far to find it. And I guess that church must have a really high steeple.

Lord, since I am so short, I suppose I am safe, but, just in case, I read further and was advised that "tall trees attract flashes of lightning, so it is safer to seek shelter under a low thorn bush." A low thorn bush? That doesn't sound very safe to me.

In spite of all this new knowledge, I still love to watch a storm and the dramatic lightning flashes from the safety of my front window. And I am grateful when "lightning strikes me" with the answer to a problem or an idea for a new book or even how to fix something "different" for dinner.

Lord, there have been a lot of "storms" in my life, but it wasn't your fault. I often did a good job of stirring them up all by myself. And you always helped me weather them and sometimes even to come up with a rainbow at the end. So thank you, Lord, for that. As I age, Lord, when I am tempted to live in the past, help me remember all the wonderful good days and never dwell on any of those storms in the past. Better yet, remind me to live in the *now*, to thank you for these bonus days and the excitement of always finding new reasons to enjoy and appreciate the wonder of your amazing world.

When you're dragging

Dear Lord, today some friends and I were talking about the terrible drug problems today and yesterday. Someone said, "Oh, I had a terrible drug problem in my teen years, and it was because of my parents. I was *drug* to go to church every Sunday, no matter what. I was *drug* to have dinner with the family and go to family reunions. I was *drug* to help friends or neighbors who had no one to help them mow the lawn or shovel snow. And now I am so grateful my *drug* problem gave me the good habits I live by today."

OK, Lord, there's a big difference between drug and dragging, but when I'm dragging, I like to think about the way my growing-up years were filled with rules and how irritating they were then, but how grateful I am for the way they led me to where I am today.

When I hear the news about all the sadness in today's world, I could feel dragged out, thinking we are doomed. Then I look around at some of the young families I know and how they are dragging their children to live by the rules and praying that they will carry the closeness of a caring family into the future.

So, Lord, thank you for reminding me of that today, when I was in dire danger of dragging around all day, burdened by the bad or sad news in the world at large. Thank you for the young'uns in my extended family who give me so much joy. Give me the courage to try to talk to them about the drug dangers today and the rewards in the future of following family rules. I know they may think it's a drag to be lectured, so give me the best words to use.

I've heard that praying for others is always a good way to forget your own worries and stop dragging around. So, Lord, whenever I have a draggy day, remind me to use that time to pray for those who are fighting drug problems. Guide them, Lord, and touch them with the knowledge of your love and care.

And thank you, Lord, that my knees may be wobbly but they are still strong enough to kneel in prayer.

When it's a bad hair day

Dear Lord, I'm ashamed to admit it, but I actually feel better when my hair looks good. So when I'm having a bad hair day, I'm having a bad day. I know, I know—it's just vanity, and it's shallow to even think about it when there are so many more important things to think about. But I was spoiled because for many years I could just run a comb through my hair and it would fall into place as ordered. It wasn't long, movie-style hair but it *was* wash and wear. No curlers or fancy styling needed. Then as I got older and fatter, it got thinner and crankier. I had heard the old saying "hair today, gone tomorrow," but I didn't think it would happen to me.

OK, Lord, I don't know why I'm talking to you about this. There is nothing in the Bible that says good hair leads to good spirituality, although it does mention Samson having a really bad hair day.

Well, I'm going to have to stop worrying about what's on the outside of my head and wonder about what's inside. I should try to comb out all the worrying that is unnecessary, all the irritations that are only temporary, all the criticisms I am tempted to make about others, all the tiredness that is there because I have stupidly chosen to try to do too much in too little time or I have chosen to do nothing when I should be doing something.

Oh Lord, this is going to take a lot of restyling—not of my hair, but of my inner head and my inner self. So maybe with your help, as usual, I will be able to stop wasting time troubling about the little things in my life and more time trying to solve the big hairy, scary ones. But I'll have to start that tomorrow, because right now I have to leave for an appointment to get my hair cut; and while I'm there I'll buy some of that extra-super-hold hairspray. It probably won't help my hair, but maybe, Lord, it will remind me to hold tighter to those good resolutions.

When listening

Dear Lord, recently I've been eavesdropping—but not on purpose. I was taught to not eavesdrop because it's impolite and it can also be dangerous. You might hear something you were not supposed to know, and that could lead to trouble. Besides, it's against the law—the "be polite to others" law. However, it seems like everywhere I go—grocery, doctor's office, post office, restaurant—someone with a phone glued to his or her ear is talking loud enough for all to hear. They could be revealing national secrets or family secrets, but they evidently don't mind sharing the conversation.

Well, Lord, I know some conversations are trivial enough to share with anyone, even those who don't want to share. But all this bad lack of phone manners makes me think of real listening.

Many people today are not just impolite. They have also forgotten the rules of listening. In a real conversation, when someone is talking to you about something that is important to them, it should be important to you. And you should really listen instead of thinking about something else or what you plan to say next. When you're old, it's especially important to listen carefully so people won't think you missed the message because you are hard of hearing. You can buy a hearing aid to improve that. But it can be embarrassing to admit you are just hard of listening.

Lord, everyone is so busy today that there's little time for real "talk." But the art of listening is one to be cherished. If you give someone the gift of your total presence, they may realize they are important to you and you truly care about whatever they are trying to tell you.

So, Lord, I know I have taken a lot of your time, but I always feel you are really listening and you care. Talk is cheap, but real listening and real prayer are priceless.

Being lured by a rocker

Dear Lord, do you realize how dangerous a rocker can be? The young folk often get lured by rock concerts, rock music, and rock stars. I get lured by the rocking chair in the family room.

In the morning, I often stumble around to put out the mail, bring in the newspaper, go to the kitchen to get the coffee started, and then search through the fridge or the pantry to try to find something to go with the coffee. But as I move about I can see that rocking chair in the family room calling to me. I know if I let myself take my cup of coffee and sink into the soft recesses of this padded rocker, I will soon be rocking to the morning news show on TV or grabbing a pen to work the day's crossword puzzle or snuggling in to read a few chapters of the book I just got from the library. And when I look at the clock, it will be lunch time.

It isn't just the morning either, Lord. At any time of day, I have to be alert to the danger. I have to be careful to get chores done, errands run, and something defrosted for dinner before that chair beckons again. People used to make jokes about old folks in their rockers. I thought that was funny until I was one.

Well, Lord, maybe I can excuse this recent happening by calling the rocking back and forth my daily exercise routine. Or I could say it is my idea of transcendental meditation, so I could claim it as a spiritual exercise.

Anyway, Lord, it is a quiet spot where I can close my eyes while I rock and send messages to you. And I can be careful not to overdo the rocking, so it will be a compliment when someone tells me, in surprise, "You're *off* your rocker!"

A trip to the moon

Dear Lord, I love that old song with the words "fly me to the moon," but now I discover that such a trip might not be as romantically heavenly as I imagined. I just read an article about the space program and how they have learned that the human body does best on earth, not in space. Since a human being is about sixty percent water, strange things happen when that body runs away from home.

It seems that in the free fall of space, body fluids float up into the head and the chest. Faces puff, and heads swell. Legs lose strength, and even eyeballs sometimes become a bit squashed. Although I no longer yearn to fly to the moon, Lord, I can still identify with being in space since this sounds just like how I sometimes feel before I get my coffee or tea in the morning.

Lord, I know this isn't a joking situation. These are serious problems that NASA continually works on, and they have already solved some of them. But NASA officials speak of the "unknown unknowns"—unforeseen problems that might catch them by surprise. Again, Lord, seniors can identify with living in that "alien territory," wondering what's around the corner.

Well, Lord, I never expected to have anything in common with the astronauts, but that song phrase "fly me to the moon" is one that often gets stuck in my swollen head. I don't remember the rest of the song, but I think it was about being with the stars and visiting Jupiter and Mars. Then it ends happily, saying "hold my hand," and I like that. Whenever I have a "senior moment," I don't have to fly to the moon to ask you to hold my hand, Lord. I know you will be with me when I have to visit and conquer all the "alien" challenges of seniority. Thanks for being my travel companion.

When questioning

Dear Lord, little kids have lots of questions, and we don't always have answers. But senior citizens have lots of questions too. Am I getting too old to drive, play golf, go to a movie, eat lunch out, tell silly jokes, dress young, sing loud, have the TV on too loud, mow the lawn, plant seeds for next year (when I may not be here then), cook, or give advice? Oh, and does my doctor know what he is doing to care for my health?

Well, Lord, we are sounding like the kids, with lots of questions and not many answers. Then, today, I picked up a book that was supposed to have "conversation starters." It asked questions that might start a conversation—or end one. "What was the happiest day in your life, and how did you spend it?" "Who is your favorite relative, and why?" "What is the luckiest thing that ever happened to you?" "What age have you liked best so far?" "What do you remember about your eighth-grade school year?" "What frightens you?"

"If you could do it all again, what three things would you change?"

Actually, I never have had too much trouble

starting a conversation—only in ending it. As you know too well, Lord, when I get started, I can go on and on. But for a while today, that little book had me scratching my head trying to answer all the questions by myself. But then I sensed a change in the atmosphere, a different odor.

Before I picked up that book, I had put on a pot of green beans to simmer for supper. I should have learned a long time ago that I should never put anything on the stove to cook and then sit down with a book. Now the beans are in the trash, and I spent a half hour scrubbing out black spots; but good news: I think I saved the pot!

Now, Lord, I have a new question for that list— "What is the stupidest thing you have done recently?" You and I know the answer.

Getting surprised

Dear Lord, today I went to a funeral and came home with a recipe! What a happy surprise. The lady who died was known far and wide for being a great cook as well as a great person, great mother, and great friend. Her children and grandchildren had put together a program for the funeral, with the prayers and songs for the Mass, but also photos of her as a child, a graduate, a newlywed, and with her many grandchildren. They added a tribute thanking their parents for teaching them the value of hard work and the importance of family. And then, on the last page, they added one of her favorite recipes.

Lord, funerals can be more difficult for people of a certain age. If one was close to the deceased, or even just an acquaintance, you have a feeling of loss as you say the last good-bye to someone of your generation. This funeral was sad, but also happy in a way as the little booklet reminded you of the many ways this lady had used her years in special ways. And the recipe left you feeling that you were taking a bit of her along home with you.

Dear Lord, as the days dwindle down to a precious few, help us all to relive the happy times, make amends for any sorrow we may have caused others, and open each new day as we would a gift box. It may not be exactly what we had hoped to find in the box, but help us rejoice in the gift and make the most of it. And, Lord, thank you for all the happy surprises you send us—even at a funeral.

Let there be light

Dear Lord, today I am being grateful for something in my house that is small and ordinary and underappreciated until it's really needed.

Last night, as you know, Lord, we were snowed in and the temperature was below zero for the first time in my memory. I was all snuggled in for a cozy winter night, ready to watch a favorite TV show, when suddenly I was in total darkness. Oh no! No electricity.

After stumbling around in the dark, I found my little miracle item—the flashlight! It helped me find the phone so I could report the outage and hear the electric company's recording that said service would be back on in a few hours. As I put on an extra blanket, I began thinking about all the underappreciated, everyday things like my flashlight, but also the many everyday people who are underappreciated most of the time.

So I thank you, Lord, for people who will climb up a pole to fix a wire when the temperature's below zero, drive a snowplow in the middle of the night to clear the streets for morning traffic, pick up the trash set out in a snowdrift, clean out a sewer, repair potholes, and all those difficult jobs that are expected but often underappreciated. Since I'm not likely to get a chance to thank any of them in person, I can only be more aware of the unknown people who make my life more comfortable and ask you to help them, Lord, and bless them.

But back to that flashlight. Just like me, it's old-fashioned. Maybe I should have a laser light for blackouts. But I'm happy with what I have—almost as happy as the folks in 1901 when the flashlight first appeared. Yes, Lord, I looked it up and read that this "latest modern convenience" was a big hit. An ad for this amazing new invention even suggested that this portable electric lamp would be valuable for the everyday traveler—in a berth on a railway car at night or in a stateroom on a steamship.

Now I'm not likely to need my flashlight in a railway car at night or in a stateroom on a steamship, but it sure was welcome in my little subdivision house on a snowy night. So thanks again, Lord, for my underappreciated marvel that "lets there be light" when needed. And please remind me to do the same whenever I am needed.

Brrr! On a chilly morning

Dear Lord, this morning I was groaning to my-self about the dark and stormy sky as I wriggled into my warmest jacket, scarf, gloves, and boots. Then I heard my teenaged grandson rousing. He opened one sleepy eye and said, "Going to church, Grandma?" When I answered yes, he mumbled: "Please tell God I said hello."

Hmmm. That changed my mood a bit. As I struggled into church and knelt for a quiet weekday morning Mass, I kept thinking of my grandson's message. As I often do, I felt so blessed and grateful, Lord. As old as I am, I can still dare the weather, drive myself out into the world, and share prayer with others. And now I can also re-joice that I have a not-yet-grown grandson who evidently feels like he is on speaking terms with you, since he feels comfortable in sending you a message! So hello, Lord, hello, hello.

I guess we old-timers grew up speaking to you in more formal ways, saying prayers with dignified terms and maybe even misunderstanding some of the words (like begotten or incarnate). Many of those old prayers are still meaningful and reverent, and I still love them and use them—and they come in handy when I can't think of anything else to say. But in today's ever-changing world, I think maybe we seniors could spend a bit more time expanding our prayer vocabulary—or maybe sometimes even shortening it.

Lord, after we give you our daily lists of complaints, worries, pains, and requests, instead of using pre-packaged prayers, we seniors might treat you like we do our other friends. We could just chat comfortably about nothing and everything, laugh at something silly, or explore a new way to fix an old recipe or a new way to solve an old problem.

Obviously, Lord, that's the kind of prayer *this* senior usually prays. And when I don't have time to chitchat, now I can remember my grandson's message and simply say, "Hello, Lord, hello."

Of shells, hermits, and woodpeckers

Dear Lord, I've been working on my overstuffed
bookcase today, clearing out and throwing out
(a chore I hate), but as I thumb through the old
books, I have learned some amazing things. It
seems that giant clam shells were once used as
holy water fonts in European churches. And giant
land tortoise shells were once used for bathtubs.
From holy water to bath water. Who knew?

Then there's the inventive hermit crab. Since
they have no shells of their own to protect their
soft vulnerable bodies from enemies, they "bor-
row" the cast-off shells of other sea creatures. And
if they can't find one, they have been known to
make their home in such other castoffs as empty
coconut shells or even soup cans. Sounds like me
making a casserole. When I don't have the proper
ingredient, I just throw in whatever I can find in
the fridge!

Next I learned the answer to the question "why
doesn't a woodpecker get a headache since it is
always hammering its head into the hard wood of
a tree?" It seems that the woodpecker's skull bones
have lots of holes in them and these spaces act

as shock absorbers. Hmmm…I can identify with that too.

I'm too often sticking my nose in where it does not belong or hammering my head against a wall looking for the solution to a problem. But I still get a headache, so those people who have suggested I have holes in my head were wrong. No shock absorbers there.

Well, Lord, I have enjoyed learning about the creatures you made, but I will never get this chore done if I don't stop reading and start dusting and pitching. But I will probably be reminded of the clams, tortoises, and woodpeckers when I make a casserole or hit my head against a stone wall or splash myself with bath water or holy water!

What can a pedicure cure?

Dear Lord, for most of my life I never knew anyone personally who got pedicures. I thought only movie stars or really rich people did that. Then I started hearing how a group of friends would have a "girls' night out" party and go together to get manicures and pedicures for fun. And when there was a wedding, the bride and bridesmaids might get pedicured. But most of my friends were non-pedicure people. At least, that's what I thought.

Then, Lord, you might have noticed the day in spring when I got out the polish to make my feet beautiful for summer sandals and swimming pools, but suddenly realized my old bones must have gotten frozen because I couldn't reach my feet. I had always considered myself to be spry and spunky, so I quickly stood up and did the old exercise of bend-over-and-touch-your-feet—and I couldn't do it! I was so shocked to get this new getting-old symptom that I called a friend to report my emergency. She laughed and said, "Well, just go get a pedicure! I'll give you the name of the place where I've been going for a couple years, since the same thing happened to me."

After that, I found out that several of my friends were regular clients of pedicure places, but it was a subject that we just never thought to talk about before. Now I am not ashamed to talk about it, because I have discovered that pedicures *can* cure. You can just pack up your troubles and sit quietly with your feet in warm swirling water as you relax totally while a very nice person pampers your feet and turns them into something you won't have to be ashamed of when you take them out in public.

So thank you, Lord, for all the good pedicurists. Thank you that I have enough pocket money to afford this luxury. And thank you that this is one time that I don't have to take a battery of tests or swallow a bottle full of pills in order to get a delightful, old-age "cure."

When the saints come...

Dear Lord, today I am thinking about the saints.
I guess we all have our favorites. I have a short
list that includes St. Bernadette, of course, and
St. Anthony, whom I need more every day since
I keep losing things and he keeps finding them.
I should include St. Monica, since she was such
a patient, long-suffering wife and mother, but I
can't really identify with her since I have not been
either of those things. And her once-bad son has
risen to such heights that I've always thought
he was above my spiritual level. But today I read
something he said that speaks to lowly me.

St. Augustine asked, "What does love look like?"
And then his answer was not in flowery language.
He simply said, "Love has hands to help others. It
has eyes to see misery and want. It has ears to hear
the sighs and sorrows of others. That's what love
looks like."

At first, we seniors might think this means we
should run away to the missions in a far-flung
country, but we're too old for that kind of travel.
We might think he means we should volunteer
to serve at a soup kitchen, but some of us have an

achy back, shaky hands, or really bad knees, so we might not be much help.

I think maybe St. Augustine might be telling us just to be on the alert, ready to use our eyes and ears to notice when someone we know—or even someone we only "know-of"— is hurting physically, mentally, or financially. Then we should use our heads and our hands to find some practical way we could show our love—with a call, a card, a casserole, a pie, an invitation to come for tea and talk, or whatever small or large help we can afford to offer.

Of course, I could be wrong, Lord. Maybe St. Augustine had higher hopes for better answers to his question, "What does love look like?"

I'll think about that some more today, Lord— and I'll get back to you.

Going bananas

Dear Lord, today I am thinking of the corny co-median who once said, "I am so old, I never buy green bananas." I can identify with that some days, thinking I am getting so fragile that I may not last long enough for a banana to ripen. But most days, I buy one beautiful, perfectly ripe banana and look forward to enjoying it before it begins to "age." Today, the banana I bought yesterday looked like the most perfect one I ever saw—firm, smooth, and just the spotless ripe shade of yellow, like the ones in pictures of a fruit bowl. Then I peeled it, and the whole inside was brown and in-edible! Can't I count on anything being the same anymore?

Lord, there were already enough things that have changed in my aging life. Instead of dashing about, I have to walk more slowly and carefully so I won't fall down and break something. I can't do all the garden chores I always loved unless I hire some help. I can't turn on the TV without expect-ing to be shocked instead of entertained.

Yes, Lord, I do remember to be thankful that I am still able to do most of the things I *want* to do and most of the things I *don't want* to do (clean house, wash dishes, take out the garbage).

And, yes, Lord, I do know that sometimes change is good for you but sometimes too much of a good thing is too much. So help me to adjust and be more grateful than gripeful. And forgive me for complaining to you about something as trivial as a banana gone bad. In spite of all the changes that are driving me bananas, I know that I am truly blessed. Thanks, Lord, thanks.

The days are getting shorter

Dear Lord, I like Daylight Savings Time because I love it when the days are getting longer and I feel like I have so much more time to do all the things I want to do. Of course I know I still only have twenty-four hours in each day, but it just seems happier. Maybe that's because I don't like to hear anything that has to do with the word *short*. I hate when I get caught short of money or shortsighted or short-winded. Sometimes I have felt guilty about my shortcomings or got lost when I tried a shortcut. But maybe I hate the word *short* because I once thought of myself as tall and willowy but now I feel embarrassed by being so short.

Lord, I can't reach the coffee cups in the cupboard now without tiptoeing—and early in the morning when I need coffee, I am barely shuffling and not in the mood to tippytoe! But I do. And I'm sure it is a sight to see. I have the plates on the lower shelf so I can quickly grab them to dish out dinner, but if there is a seldom-used bowl that I need, I have to go to the garage and drag in the step-stool. Now anyone could understand why I hate any idea of short. People used to tell me that "good things come in small packages," but they don't do that much any more, since I started stopping them with my piercing, x-ray-deadly, undo-right, evil-eye zapper.

To add to the insult, as I got older, I lost inches in height but not in width—which was definitely the wrong direction to go. But I can't complain or get any sympathy because several of my friends say they have the same "aging" problem.

Well, enough of that, Lord. I am still un-short enough to give my tall grandson a hug or to grab the best bargain at a garage sale or to reach for the last chocolate in the box. And when it comes to joy and gratefulness and appreciation for so many blessings, I seldom fall short in that.

Dear Lord, I always try to have green plants in my house, because long ago I heard something about carbon dioxide. I can't remember exactly, but it seems that we breathe out and foul the air, and green plants breathe in and clean the air; so plants help clean the house. Anything that helps clean the house is on my gotta-have list. My mother was inventive, creative, a great cook, and a lot of fun when taking a trip, but she would never get a grade-A for housecleaning. I inherited the gene.

On the side of our house where you let the sun shine in, Lord, I try to have plants in every window. They flourish there, so they must be happy, but they always grow toward the window as though they are trying to get out—and some days I can identify with that, since I am happy inside, but as I get older and slower, I often feel the urge to escape for just a little while.

But, Lord, sometimes when I do escape, the plants give me another reason to feel guilty (as though I didn't have enough reasons already). When I am back home, I will suddenly look more closely at a plant, and its leaves will look pale and sad—and I realize I have not watered them on time. Shame, shame on me. Here they are, working to keep my house air clean, and I forget that they are totally dependent on me for water. The outside plants can hope for a sudden rain shower, but the insiders have only me! Just like people, they can survive without food but not without water.

So, Lord, I know this is something silly again to be talking to you about, but it does make me realize that I should not just sit around with my cup of tea and crossword puzzles. No matter how feeble-minded I get, I should still be responsible to take care of the maintenance of myself, my plants, my house, and my spirituality.

And I should probably look up that info about carbon dioxide, so I can pass it on more sensibly.

The missing link

Dear Lord, there may be a lot of missing links in
my life or my family, but the one that troubles me
most these days is the one in my head. I'll be right
in the middle of telling some exciting (!?) story,
and suddenly the next word gets stuck. I stumble
around and substitute another word, but it is very
aggravating. I was worried about it until a friend
told me she was having the same problem. Then I
read a humorous definition of the word *synonym*
as "a word you use when you suddenly can't think
of the word you meant to use." So I guess this
missing link syndrome is spreading.

Lord, when I talk to you, as I do so often, I sometimes want to find a word good enough to tell you
how grateful or joyful or amazed I am with all the
wonderful things you have put into my life and
all the bonus years you have gifted me with, but I
know I could never find any words good enough to
use. But you can see inside my head and my heart,
and you know what I want to say.

Unfortunately, my friends sometimes can't see
inside me as well as you can, so they must get very
irritated at my loss of a word since I never ever was

at a loss for words when I was younger. But I can't blame everything on aging, so maybe I could avoid this if I didn't talk so fast or so much. Also unfortunately, that's probably not going to happen.

So, Lord, bless my friends for their patience when I start to stumble around looking for that missing word. And help me find enough synonyms to get all those exciting (!?) stories told before I forget them!

Focus pocus

Dear Lord, I've often heard the term "hocus-pocus," usually referring to something to do with a magic trick or a flimflam of some sort. Now it seems the new magic word for seniors is *focus*. I read an article about senior driving, and it tells me to focus only on what I am doing and try to sharpen my driving skills. I hear someone on radio or TV speaking about senior memory loss. She says I may not be forgetting things, I just have to focus more on remembering names, instructions, etc. I visit with a friend, and she reports how she is working hard to learn the focus lesson.

Lord, at first, it sounded to me like a lot of focus pocus, and in the past I would have just laughed about it. But since I am such a vulnerable senior now, I took a second look. I really have been a bit lax when driving—concentrating on something interesting on the radio, looking out the window at a pretty view or an estate sale sign. So I try now to really focus on driving only; it seems to help, and I feel more in control, which sort of even makes me feel younger.

Now, the computer is another problem. When

it goes kerflooey, I ask my son. He moans and shows me the simple thing I need to do to fix it, and I am sure I will never forget what I need to do. The next time it happens, I can't believe I forgot that simple thing, so I hit a button here and there and really make it worse. Then I ask my grandson. Now I focus on what he is doing, and I write down each step in a little book I leave right next to the computer. And the next time there's a kerflooey, I read the instructions and do not let myself hit any buttons—and it works!

Of course, there are still some things I am not focusing on—the cobweb in the corner, the pile of laundry not done, the stack of new recipes still not tried—but I'll work my way to them. And yes, Lord, I should focus a bit more on prayer, but seriously speaking, this focus thing really might help me age a bit more carefully. Maybe focus is not hocus-pocus.

Out but in the season

Dear Lord, today there is no tree growing in the middle of my living room, no colorful sparkling lights sprinkled through the neighborhood, no sound of tiny hoofs on the roof. But I am in the Christmas spirit. That's because, after New Years Day, I set aside all the Christmas cards until I had "time" to look through them again—and today I finally came across where I put them, so I am making the time.

And today is just the day to do it because it snowed last night and my yard looks just like a Christmas card. So I'm pretending my cup of hot tea is wassail and I am enjoying looking at the Christmas photos of families, seeing how the "little children" have changed since last year. This year, some were pictured on their college graduation day, some on their wedding day, and some with the cutest new baby. Yes, they too are growing older, but in such nice ways. Seeing them so bright and beautiful should maybe make me feel old, but instead it just fills me with delight.

I also like looking again at the wonderful variety of cards and the little handwritten hellos. And, yes, I also appreciate the Christmas newsletters that some friends send. It gives me a chance to connect over the miles, finding out what has happened in their lives through the year.

Lord, I know some people think those letters are a bore. As you know, I am one of the boring people who keeps sending them anyway because I like to get some back. I guess that's why I keep talking to you so much. I like to get something back. And I always do. I hear a song. I see a feisty little bird munching on the bread I threw on my snowy patio. I get a hug. I am warmed with a cup of soup. I find a book I really want to read. I get a phone call from a friend. I come across an old holy card with an old prayer I love. And I know you are with me. Always.

My favorite joints

Dear Lord, I am giggling today about all the "joints" I have enjoyed through the years. In my teens, I loved the Candy Shop. I don't know why it was called that, since we never bought candy there, but they had the best homemade ice cream and delicious "petite" sandwiches, unlike the "everything-but-the-kitchen-sink" style today. But my favorite was their special, original, red, carbonated drink that, sipped through a straw, was like no drink I have found since.

Then there was a restaurant joint that somehow was in a renovated streetcar on a side street. They didn't serve fancy food, but they had a simmered steak that was better than anything I've had in today's fanciest steak houses. And there was a soda shop that had a "Hawaiian Delight" drink that was in a frosted tall glass with sweetened, crushed pineapple in the bottom, topped with grape juice. I know it sounds weird, but I was always so happy when I had a little extra change so I could order it instead of a cola.

Oh, and through the years, I have to admit there have been some favorite "gin joints" like

Humphrey Bogart talked about in the old movies. I seldom had any gin there, but I did have lots of good times with old friends.

Well, Lord, today my favorite joints are the ones that don't hurt when I use them—the knee, the hip, the jaw, the elbow, and some that I don't even have a name for. The bad news is that most of them do hurt when I use them, but the good news is that sometimes they don't hurt, or at least not as bad. And I am so grateful that they are still working at all after all these years. So thank you, Lord, for my old, but usable joints and for all the memories of the others.

Hear ye! Hear ye!

Dear Lord, today I heard a sermon about the prophets, and I slowly realized that sometimes I act like I think *I* am a prophet. I know just what is going to happen in the future and what others should or should not do to keep it from happening or to make it happen. And soon I become a judge of others! Well, that's not good.

Thinking of the ways I have handled certain "emergencies or crises" in my own life, I am certainly not capable of giving advice or judging anyone. In the past, even when I piteously asked for your help and advice, I didn't always accept it. When I was younger, I always knew "best." Even when I secretly suspected my "judgment" might be faulty, just to show someone, I often jumped off a cliff and did not land in a field of feathers.

As I have grown older, I have been more careful around cliffs and even molehills, afraid I might trip and break something. I have even tried to be more careful in acting as judge and jury, afraid I might trip and hurt somebody else. Of course, Lord, I make this sound like a big change but it's only a small beginning. I am still in danger of opening my mouth when others would appreciate my silence. I am aware that aging may give you more wrinkles, more bad hair days, more aches, but it does not automatically give you more wisdom.

So, Lord, help me and other "gracefully aging" folks to think before we judge the young'uns. Help us share any truly helpful knowledge or experience life has given us, but only in small doses. And when we are tempted to spill out old hurts or old prejudices disguised as "helpful hints" for the young, remind us to not load this onto the next generation when we are mentioning it just to get it out of our systems.

Well, that's enough judging myself and others for today. Lord, I know you are the only true judge but you have been a wise but gentle, loving judge in my life. Help me try to follow your example.

Beautiful blooming

Dear Lord, today I went shopping at the grocery
where the first thing you see when you go into
the door is an arrangement of small, large, and
larger blooming bouquets of flowers. I love it! It
reminds me of something somebody famous once
said: "When I have a bit of money I buy books,
and if there's any money left I buy bread." Well, I
feel that same way about flowers.

It's only in recent years that the groceries where
I shop have started selling things like flowers and
greeting cards. And this grocery has the best and
brightest of both. So I chose a $3.99 bouquet and
a couple of $1.00 greeting cards and then I got
groceries and went home happy.

Lord, I always wished I could have fresh flowers
in my home, but I settled for green plants because
flowers were expensive. Now I can splurge on a
small bouquet and not feel like a spendthrift.

And when there's a special occasion like a
birthday, I can even buy the large bouquet and
take it to a friend. But I also remember a different
kind of bouquet that we used to give to friends
and family—and it didn't cost *any* money. It was a

"spiritual bouquet." I think, and hope, that today's children are still being taught to make these.

In my little box where I save some very old holy cards given to me on special occasions, there is probably a spiritual bouquet someone gave to me—a pretty card with a crayon drawing of a flower and the promise to say five Our Fathers, five Hail Marys, or maybe even a rosary for my intentions.

No matter how many prayers were promised, just the idea of someone else praying for you and your "intentions" was a very comforting gift. And I think it would be a welcome gift today too, maybe coming *from* instead of *to* a "senior," who would take the time to make a little card and say a few little prayers. Hmmm, Lord, as I'm sitting here looking at my lovely $3.99 bouquet, maybe I'll just make a spiritual bouquet for someone and get it in the mail. I hope the person I send it to thinks it's a good idea—and, Lord, I hope, and think, you will too.

Vertebrates and lepidoptera

Dear Lord, I don't usually use the proper names when I speak of the birds and butterflies that visit my patio, but they are so special that they deserve fancy names. I am always so happy when they drop in for a few minutes. We live near a lovely butterfly house where people go to watch them "come to life," flap their beautiful wings, and start to float about through a garden of greenery. And I think some of those "lepidoptera" must escape and come our way, because we have a great variety of these flying tapestries of all colors and designs lighting in our own little garden of greenery.

And the birds…oh, the birds! I read that there are 8600 species of birds! We only see a few, like the little wren that comes every spring to move back into our old birdhouse and fill our air with lovely birdsong every day. And the arrogant mockingbird that not only speaks several foreign languages but sometimes thinks he's king of the walk, ordering other birds out of his way. And the cardinals adding splashes of brilliant scarlet plumage to our modest plantings.

Sometimes we see little snowbirds and hummingbirds and blue jays, but they are so different and delightful that they could each be called a bird of paradise. Lord, thank you for putting such a variety in our world.

Even on days when no butterflies and only a few birds come to visit, my patio is the perfect place to sit and be grateful for a peaceful spot to meditate and give thanks for my long life. There have been some cloudy days and stormy nights, but there were times when life was as colorful and intricate as the pattern on a butterfly's wing, and days when I felt I had wings to fly and songs to sing. And there is still more to discover and to try to find ways to adapt and make each minute count. Thanks, Lord, thanks.

Dear Lord, as helpers in all my writings, my
bookcases are clogged with different editions of
the dictionary, encyclopedias, trivia books, etc.
But I have never owned a copy of the venerable
Oxford English Dictionary, the masterpiece of them
all. And I probably never will since the current
cost of the twenty-volume set is $995! If I had
not bought all those $9.95 books on my shelves,
maybe I could have saved up for it, but it's too late
now. Today the O.E.D. might be said to be more
revered than owned. With all the free Internet
ways today to look up, find out about, and search
for just the proper words, change is afoot at the
O.E.D. All along, its editors have been aware of
how language changes, and they have inserted
tech talk, teen talk, street talk, etc. And when pur-
ists complained, they explained that many people
don't understand that a dictionary is not meant to
define only how language *should* be used, but also
how it *is* used today.

Lord, I once read about how the plan for the
O.E.D. began in 1858, when people were asked
to send in their ideas of which words should be

included; the editors soon received thousands of little slips of paper with words written on them, mailed from all over the world. It took seventy years to choose which words to include, so the first edition didn't come out until 1928.

Lord, once again I've taken your time talking about things you already know. But you also know how fascinated I am by words and the power they have to turn a bad day into a wonderful one, or to change a happy day into a bitter one. We should be so careful and responsible in choosing the words we use every day. Please help me, Lord, and all the "talkers," to think before we speak. And when we misspeak, show us how to go back and try to heal the hurt or right the wrong.

And, Lord, you also know that I have files and desk drawers filled with little slips of paper with "ideas" I hope to use some day, or recipes I mean to make some day, or inspirational messages that I plan to use to turn me into a better person some day. The clock is ticking, so I can't count on seventy years to go through them. What should I do, Lord? Is it time to—pardon the expression—clean out those drawers?

Canes and crutches

Dear Lord, today I keep humming that song with the line, "brown paper packages tied up with string, these are a few of my favorite things." You don't see many packages wrapped up with string these days. Everything is put in plastic bags. They're nice, but I doubt anyone will write a song about them. However, the song reminded me of some things that are *not* favorites of the elder gang. I speak of canes, walkers, hearing aids, even glasses. People who obviously need glasses won't wear them, but keep squinting all the time or asking you to read a price tag for them. With all the jazzy new frames for glasses, if these folks would put on some specs, they might even look younger and see things they have been missing.

When I first needed reading glasses, I kept losing them all the time. I kept needing them, because most of my time I was reading a book, a newspaper, or a recipe, typing something on the computer, or reading prices on garage sale items So I asked the eye guy if he would give me a prescription for bifocals, using the lower part for my reading prescription and just using plain glass in the top, since I could still see distances. He did, and I've been wearing glasses all day, every day since.

Then, Lord, you remember a while back when I had a leg problem and I was limping around, one day better, one day worse. So one worse day, I decided to get out the cane I found in the back of the closet. When I walked in with a cane, everybody got all excited. "What happened? Are you OK?" If I had broken that leg or even a toe and had a cast with crutches, they would have been less surprised. People of all ages can be seen with crutches, but not canes. It's an "old" thing.

I still use that cane once in a while—if I go to a museum or have to walk a long way somewhere. It's not much help, but when people see the cane, they do offer to open doors for me and that's nice.

Well, Lord, I don't need to make a list of all senior woes for you. It's always something to patch, patch, patch. But that's OK. Patched-up jeans came in style, and all the young folks wanted them. Now, if canes, walkers, hearing aids, etc., would come into style, we seniors could start singing, "these are a few of our favorite stylish things." But I guess we better not wait for that to happen and just keep on keeping on.

Wills and liberties

Dear Lord, when I was a kid I learned about Patrick Henry, the patriot and statesman who said, "Give me liberty or give me death."

I confess I have forgotten a lot of things I was supposed to learn back then, but this one hung on. Now, recently, I heard that there is an even better quote from him. It seems that when he made out and signed his last will and testament, he said, "I have now disposed of all my property to my family. There is one thing more I wish I could give them, and that is the Christian religion. If they had that, and I had not given them one shilling, they would have been rich; and if they had not that, and I had given them all the world, they would be poor."

Lord, when we were young, we wanted to give our children all we didn't have. If we could afford it, or even if we couldn't quite afford it, we gave them bigger toys, more education, nicer vacations, and hopes for having a better life. As we get older, we may be proud that we did as much as we could, or we may wonder what we did wrong or what we could have done better. And mostly, we hope we have given our children faith in you, Lord.

Thank you for the gift of children and nieces and nephews and grandchildren. No matter how old we get, help us to be a good example to them and to show them how you can be a loving friend and loving presence if only they will open their hearts and welcome you into their lives. If and when that happens, the next generation will have discovered the true meaning of a rich inheritance.

Hold on and let go

Dear Lord, I once again heard a very old joke today, and I still laughed at it. It's the one about a guy who fell off a cliff but was able to grab onto a tree limb on his way down. He started yelling for help, saying, "Is there anybody up there?" A voice answered saying, "Yes, I am God and I will help you." The guy said, "What should I do, Lord?" and God answered, "Let go." The guy thought a minute and then said, "Is there anybody else up there?"

Lord, I'm afraid we all have had times when we didn't like the kind of help we were afraid you would suggest. And as the years add on, we are told to "hold on," to keep trying to be active and alert and hold down the fort. But we are also told that there comes a time when we have to let go of various activities or whatever we can't handle too well any more. Since we are old, we are also terribly wise, so we know we should try to do both of those things. But when you are clutching at a tree limb or the last straw, it isn't easy to do either or both.

So, Lord, I pray that you will let us know when we are supposed to hold on to the old ways and the old activities, but also tell us when the time has come for us to let go. For some, that time may come early because of illness or financial problems or just getting tired of the same old, same old. Others may be able to keep on keeping on like the Energizer Bunny. We read about the one-hundred-year-old folks who are still living happily ever after.

Well, Lord, you made all kinds of young people who grew into old age in different ways, so help us know which kind we are and when we have to hold on or let go. And, Lord, whenever that is, we will know that you will never let go of us.

Time to re-tire

Dear Lord, my elderly car is not ready to retire yet,
but it needs to be re-tired. So I recently learned
that tires are not cheap. And once you get them,
you have to have them balanced, then later rotated,
and always pumped up to the correct air pressure.
It sounds like they are a lot of trouble. But those
tires have the hard job of holding up the car and all
the stuff in it, and they have to roll around in traffic
every day, so I guess they are a bargain after all.

You could say that tires are like some elder
folk—not quite ready to retire, but needing some
maintenance. Those folk try to stay balanced, and
if they still have a good job, they hope they won't
get rotated too soon. But that air pressure is a
problem. There is no "filling station" that has air
ready to pump them up when they need it.

And most of us, whether retired or almost re-
tired, *need* it. Of course, whenever I'm around,
there's plenty of *hot* air in my house, but that is
not the kind recommended for pumping anyone
up except maybe yourself. Each person probably
has a favorite filling station to go to find a fill
up—like maybe chocolate, music, or a good book

to read. But one sure cure could be prayer. I've tried it, and it often works for me.

So, dear Lord, thanks for listening to my long prayers and for letting me still have a car, a budget that can re-tire it, and places to go with it. Forgive me for all the hot air I spread around, complaining or finding fault when my little "problems" are so much smaller than those of others. And thanks too for chocolate, music, good books, and fresh air when needed.

My kingdom for a....

Dear Lord, this morning I remembered that story about a king whose horse was lost in battle, and the king shouted, "A horse, a horse, my kingdom for a horse!" Well, I didn't need a horse today, but I felt like shouting, "A tooth, a tooth, my kingdom for a tooth."

That was stupid, since I don't have a kingdom; but I desperately needed a tooth. I had been sipping a cup of coffee and munching on a very soft piece of banana bread when suddenly I felt a rock in my mouth. It wasn't a rock or a horse. My front tooth fell out— and luckily I didn't swallow it. It was early, so I had to wait to call the dentist's office, but when I did, they said they would work me in. So off I went, looking like I was on my way to a Halloween party each time I smiled at a passerby.

Lord, I was so lucky. It was actually the cap of a tooth that had been worked on who-knows-how-long-ago, and the dentist said he could just glue the cap back on, and he did. And I went home looking a bit less like the Wicked Witch of the West.

As a senior, I have become more aware of chewing, walking, breathing, bending, reaching—and all the body parts necessary to keep me able to do such things. Thank you, Lord, for helping me to find spare parts (like the cap) and for "mechanics" who know how to replace them. I could probably use some new spark plugs, but my headlights and horn get me most places I want to go. I'm grateful for that, since I don't have the household budget of a kingdom to spend on new parts.

Dear Lord, today I was reminded of an old story about a shepherd leading his flock. They came to a shallow stream they needed to cross, but the sheep were suddenly frightened and would not step into the water, no matter what the shepherd did to lead them. There was a baby lamb in the flock, and the shepherd very gently picked up the baby and carried it across. When the mother saw her baby on the other side—although she was afraid like the others—she stepped into the water and crossed to be with her baby. And the other sheep followed her lead.

Well, for most of us who have lived a long life, we have played each part in this story. At home or in business, we have been the one trying to lead the "flock" in the direction we felt they needed to go. When they refused, we tried a new approach, and if we found a proper one, it worked. Or we have been the baby lamb—too young, too inexperienced, too weak to do anything to help ourselves until a wise parent, teacher, or friend gently "carried" us to safety. Or we have been the mother (or the father), afraid like the rest of the flock, but ready to take any steps necessary to help or save that child. And then, of course, we have all been the flock frozen with fear until we saw it was OK to go ahead and step into the stream.

Lord, I can remember so many times when I had one or the other of those experiences. So many times fear stopped or delayed the step I needed to take. But I was so blessed. I always thought I could go to you and ask for direction. Some people say they are frozen through "fear of the Lord." I was never afraid of you, Lord, so that's why I could always ask for help. Even then, sometimes I either misunderstood your advice or chose stupidly to ignore it. But I always finally figured it out, gave in, and followed your directions instead of mine, knowing you would try to show me the way by gently carrying me across.

Thank you, Lord, and please help anyone who is frozen with fear of the Lord today. Let them know you are listening and always ready to carry them too.